Aella Greene

Conflict and Conquest

And Other Poems

Aella Greene

Conflict and Conquest
And Other Poems

ISBN/EAN: 9783744705110

Printed in Europe, USA, Canada, Australia, Japan

Cover: Foto ©Thomas Meinert / pixelio.de

More available books at **www.hansebooks.com**

CONFLICT AND CONQUEST

AND OTHER POEMS,

— BY —

AELLA GREENE,

AUTHOR OF "RIVER, BIRD AND STAR,"
AND "JOHN PETERS."

Published in 1897.

THE COTTAGER COMPANY, PRINTERS,

ATHOL, MASS.

In Remembrance of
Friendships whose Shining has Dispelled
the darkness of many a
Gloomy Day.

CONTENTS.

CONFLICT AND CONQUEST.

I.

IN days when fiends who came to earth
  For purposes of blood and dearth
Found those who were alert and brave
To meet whatever fight they gave,
The devils, wroth to think it true
'Twas long since fiends a pilgrim slew,
In hellish conclave planned to slay
The mortal first to dare their fray,
When, soon, insatiate, they, again,
Should seek and vex the haunts of men.
And Doubt, the monster known as Fear,
Sat eminent, and Hate was near,
With score of impish jealousies.
And sneaking Slander, versed in lies,
And Selfishness and Envy came,
With lesser fiends that have no name.
And Fear they chose as chief and well
Attired with mail annealed in hell !
They armed him with a heavy blade
That seemed for some dread business made ;
And chains they took with which to bind,
If so the monster felt inclined,
The mortal he should give affray
And torture ere he deigned to slay.

Thus furnished, he was earthward sent;
And with him minor demons went,
The champion fiend to serve and guard,
That mortals should not press too hard;
While Fear, himself, equipped for fight,
Appeared enough a host to fright.

When nearing earth the fiends could see
A man of pilgrim panoply,
Who upward fared o'er desert strand
Which downward slopes to demonland.
Across this desert fevered airs
Alternate sweep with chill despairs,
Each zephyr trembling with the moan
Of those the fiends have overthrown.
And here as long as suits the sprites
Victorious in their earthly fights
Their victims writhe in fiercest pains,
Close kept by fiends upon the plains.

Meanwhile the demons poise above
The place where they with pilgrims strove,
And taunt them with a fiendish laugh
And water held too far to quaff.
They plunge the wretches then below,

To drink of an intenser woe
Within the confines of a pit
Of which description is not fit.
The equal words were so severe
That even stoics who should hear,
Though gifted with unearthly might,
Would shriek and shiver in affright!
How came this man amid the dearth
Of that wild outward strand of earth,
Whence came he there, and why, to dwell,
And dwelt how long, needs not to tell;
Needs not to name the fates that strove—
Misfortune if to honest love,
Or if 'twas other grief that drove.
What angel cheered him is not known,
What airs salubrious from what zone,
What heavenly radiance from on high,
What happy bird of sunniest sky!
Nor whence his blade, nor whence his shield,
If angels or if men, annealed;
Nor whence the pilgrim raiment given,
That seemed of earth while, still, of heaven!

Some spirit or some bird of song
He must have heard, so brave and strong

Fared he the desert way along.
If briefest halt he made for rest,
The faster onward then he pressed,
Till breezes muttered to his ear
The hate of fiends approaching near.
And still the pilgrim kept his way,
Undaunted by the dawning fray
That he discovered in their eyes
Who came his progress to surprise.
And when the guards began assault
They paid most dearly for the fault.
For many imps he conquered soon,
And others routed till the noon.
Then on the scene the chief appeared,
Brandished his blade and loudly jeered.
Yet he so fenced the blows away
Whom Fear had thought an easy prey,
Half down the sky the lustre stood,
Ere fiendish blade had tasted blood.
And, with his wound, courageous grew
The man, the conflict to renew.
And yet, though well he bore the blows
The fiend laid on whose fury rose
Till fiercely glowed his face with rage
That such brave war the man should wage,

As o'er the scene the anxious sky
Noted the passioned hours go by,
The warrior's surely ebbing might
Showed he must yield, at last the fight.
And nature sighed in grief to see
The fiend was gaining mastery !

When sad the sunset closed the day
That trembled with the mighty fray,
Deep-hewn by Fear and left in bands,
To pine upon the desert sands,
His wounds proclaimed that long and well
The hero battled   ere he fell.
Yet he, though brave, was vanquished still,
With spirit crushed and broken will,
And fitting were the sombre skies
In which it seemed no sun could rise !
Responsive to the sufferer's moans,
The wild waste thrilled with thunder tones ;
Yet rains blessed not those desert airs—
There are no tears for some despairs !

Yet no despairs but timely deed
Of kindness meets the spirit's need,

And wakes the bird of hope to sing,
That earthward calls those swift of wing.
And, trembling at that song of cheer,
The victor fiends that hover near
To taunt persistent every sigh
That speaks the sufferer's wish to die,
Aware the song portends at hand
The powers their might cannot withstand,
Forget their glee and in affright
Quick speed them through the murky night !

RESCUE.

A stranger o'er that desert way
    Came where the panting sufferer lay,
Knelt like a brother at his side
And tried to staunch the ruddy tide,
And, ere the wounded man could ask,
Proffered him water from his flask.
The hero drank, his thirst to slake,
And thus, in heartfelt whispers, spake :

"Grateful that Providence did send,
I thank thee for thy coming, friend,
The sentry imps Fear stationed here
Were quick to flee when cam'st thou near.
He gat him elsewhere with his blade,
And must have other havoc made.
Search that, and give thy blessing there
Till angels shall relieve thy care.
And I am safe, since hope doth sing
That timely aid from heaven shall bring.
For spoke an angel unto me
When pined my soul in misery,
And said if on the upward way
I met a demon in affray
And bravely battled in the fight
The skies would honor me with might
And send a bird whose tuneful cheer
The listening angels always hear,
And hearing, swift and gladly fly
With blessings from the gracious sky.
Remembering this, I tried to wage
The war against the monster's rage !"

And through that midnight to the plains,
To oint his wounds and loose his chains,

Whom first a human friend addressed,
Whom first a human hand had blessed,
The bright ones of the pitying skies
Came swift of wing for such emprise,
And clusters brought from heavenly vine,
High-cultured for the feasts divine.
Of these he ate, and peaceful slept.
The while the angels vigils kept,
Till flushing bright with rosy flame,
O'er eastern hills the morning came,
And Heaven in high approval smiled
On every feature of the wild !
The desert greened to grassy glades,
Wherein to cadence of cascades,
By joyous brooks, and blessed with shades,
That, frequent as the hero's needs,
Were flecked along the flowery meads,
His heart harmonious with the day,
He fared with gladscmeness his way,
To each entrancing scene and song
Awake, and yet sustained and strong,
And not o'ercome by sudden boon,
That still came not the least too soon—
Surveying, with emotions due,
Earth all the same, yet grandly new !

Yet that bright scene was in the land
Of barrenness, the desert strand
That downward slopes unto the dearth
Upon the arid verge of earth.
And desert still the place remains,
And desert all the neighboring plains.
But there, within that wilderness,
Where pined the pilgrim in distress,
A man and angels came to bless.
So, honored, there, of earth and skies,
The pilgrim sees through visioned eyes ;
And unto him the desert seems
A land of verdure and of streams.

VICTORY.

HIS struggles gave the pilgrim ken
    Aright to read despairing men ;
And wishing that they dare to try
The upward road from misery,
He sought to lead them from their woes,
And rash the fiend that dared oppose.

If any one his course withstood
He found a blade to drink his blood.

The trusty steel would never fail
To journey swift through hardest mail
Which devils wear when earthward sent,
The hardest which the fiends invent
Who study long and ponder well
The ores and alchemies of hell !

Once, only once, did Fear essay
To re-enact the first affray.
It was one morn when o'er the strand
The pilgrim upward led a band,
That he espied his former foe
Equipped from armories below
And posing in effrontery
Where erst he practiced cruelty.
Though guarded by a retinue
And dread-inspiring to the view,
The monster little trembling caused,
And though the pilgrim briefly paused,
' Twas but for an assuring word
That heartened well the band who heard.
To heaven they sent the sincere prayer
That ever finds acceptance there.

Meanwhile their leader forward went,
To ascertain the fiend's intent,
And, if his presence warfare meant,
To trust the skies and do his best
The monster's boldness to arrest.
The blade he bore appeared so weak
A fairy's gentlest touch would break ;
And still there slumbered in that steel
The might to make the monster reel,
Fourfold of what it had the day
When first it dared a demon's fray.
The skies impart to every one
Who have for others bravely done,

Quadruple power for any fight
They wage thereafter for the right.
This well the pilgrim understood ;
And yet he had no warlike mood,
Nor thirst for even fiendish blood.
And meek he seemed, and was, and mild,
And seemed in prowess but a child.
But fiends could never read the face
Aright of excellence and grace.
And Fear supposed an easy fight
Would put the man in sorry plight.

True, he had never yet forgot
How angels drove him from the spot,
When erst against the man he fought
And such terrific havoc wrought ;
Nor yet forgot the song that brought
Those angels earthward from the skies
Before whom every demon flies.
But greed in men or fiends will blind
And far from caution swerve the mind.
And hate beyond all other greed
Will unto wildest ventures lead.

And, guarded by an impish clan,
The fiend bore down upon the man.
Quick glowed the pilgrim then with light
Reflected from his inner might.
An instant impulse as from heaven
Inspired the dart the fiend was given,
A thrust that pierced the demon through
And sent him howling homeward, long to stay
And nurse his wounds and curse the day
He dared this pilgrim to affray.
The pigmy fiends without their chief,
'Twas scarce a skirmish and 'twas brief,

To bring the demon dwarfs to grief.
The pilgrim tossed them on his blade,
And of the swarm such pastime made
As left them silent where they fell,
And called for obsequies in hell,
When there by other imps were borne
The forms the hero's steel had torn!

MISSION AND OUTLOOK.

AND still the pilgrim, wise to cheer,
And stronger grown by fighting Fear,
Resorts unto the desert strand
That borders close on demonland.
And patient and persistent there,
To win the saddened from despair,
He rouses some to make the fight
Of struggling from their wretched plight.
But some there are no words can move,
Though spoken from a heart of love.
And who would any hopeless lead
From thence, of gentleness has need,
So worn are all from grinding cares,
So faint from starving on despairs.

And some of these are grown so weak
They scarce can think, they cannot speak ;
So weak they deem soft airs severe
And tremble if a bird they hear ;
So weak a shadow's weight would break,
So weak, who once, perchance, could take
Herculean blows, unharmed, and bear
With equipoise a world of care,
Rebuke the impudence of fate,
And quench the venomed darts of hate.
And these the pilgrim reads aright,
And kens by faith beyond the night
The summits where the splendors play,
That prophesy for them the day.
And thither, silent all the way,
Right on he leads, and looks the cheer
They, looking, beg, but dare not hear.

But walk they can, for well they know
They're faring upward from their woe.
They read it in the matchless grace
That speaks the leader's noble race,
They read it in his soldier pace,
They read it in his radiant face,
They read it in his hopeful eyes

That shine with joy of victories
And shed along the starless night
A lustre more than stellar light.

And some with speech the pilgrim cheers,
With reminiscence of the years
A stranger brightened by a deed
That met a famished sufferer's need,
A stranger by a deed of love
That brought the angels from above,
A man he had not seen before,
A man whom here he saw no more,
A stranger since ascended where
The best of bright fruitions are !
And others as he fares along
The pilgrim heartens with the song
That, caroled by the joyous bird,
The wild waste and the midnight heard
When once upon that desert way
He met a fiend in an affray
That saddened and that shook a day !

If some must halt for sleep, their rest
He sentinels and then with zest

He leads them to the mountain top
Resplendent with the morn of hope.
His chivalry the rescued learn,
And with the like emotions burn,
And with him to the plains return,
And others lead unto the heights,
To taste of hope's supreme delights.

O ! lovely hills where Edens are
Without a flaming sword to bar !
Bright summits where from dawn to star
And from the star to dawn again,
Angels descend to talk with men.
And this their message from the skies,
Faith ever true, Doubt always lies !

And ere they spread the heavenward wing
They wake their golden harps and sing
The song that charmed the pilgrim's grief
And summoned them to give relief.
And this refrain thrills through the song,
Faith always right, Doubt always wrong !

There, on the heights, the champion stands,
The love and wonder of the bands

He rescued from their foes and chains
And led o'er demon-haunted plains
Unto the hills above the airs
That sweep the region of despairs.
And there, with vision to discern
Where heaven's eternal glories burn,
He sees translated to his rest,
Crowned in the country of the blest,
Rejoicing with the sons of light,
The one who cheered his desert night !

And, hark ! what minstrelsy inspires !
Ay ! wafted from celestial choirs,
The very song that charmed the plains
When angels came to loose his chains !
They careful conned the harmonies
To aid the anthems of the skies !
And now the song which then was given
Is chanted as a hymn of heaven !
Harmonious with the rhythmic spheres
And cadence of eternal years !

FORDING AND BEYOND.

II.

"MORNING GILDS THE OTHER SIDE."

CONSTANT over death's dark river
    Shine the lustrous stars of love ;
And, to cheer the good man, hover
    Angels missioned from above.
Faith reveals to him the glories
    Of a land beyond the tide ;
Though there's darkness on the river,
    Morning gilds the other side !

Earth to him is but a province
    Of a better land that lies
Out beyond the hidden boundary
    Of this scene of mysteries.
Angels call him, and no demons
    Come to taunt with evil done,
Or, insatiate in their hatred,
    Paint a heaven he might have won.

Fearful still to ford the river !
    Seem the dark waves mountain high.
For, whatever visions promise,
    Yet to die, is still to die !

Dreaded journey ! none escape it ;
    All must go, and go one way,
Sometime go, and soon that sometime,
    None prevent it, none delay.

And that way is through the river
    Where no morning ever shone ;
And the pilgrim that way faring
    Goes at midnight, goes alone !
Be it at the break of morning,
    Seems it in a starless night ;
Be it in the gladsome summer,
    Seems it in November's blight.

Be it when by friends surrounded,
    Powerless now is friendship's hand ;
Faith inspirits, yet in going
    Fares he to an unknown land.
Other torrents he has forded
    In his travel hitherto,
Streams so deep, and swift, and wrathful,
    Only brave men venture through.

Rugged steeps his courage clambered,
    Deserts knew his blistered feet,

Found he thornfield, flint and quicksand,
    Adverse winds and biting sleet !
Now he nears the final river,
    Airs grow dense, and damp, and chill ;
Birds once vanguard here turn backward,
    He must onward, onward still !

On he fares—and why his calmness
    As the shadows round him close?
Why invincible his courage
    To the waters that oppose?
There's a hope that sings within him
    Of a land beyond the tide—
Though there's darkness on the river,
    Morning gilds the other side !

Morn of brightness ! morn of gladness !
    Morn of full revealing why
All the hardness of the journey
    To the country of the sky !
Land of morning, sweetened, brightened,
    Land of morning grown to noon,
Land of springtime grown to summer—
    Land of everlasting June !

Mountains welcome home the good man,
 Rivers give him greeting there,
And the trees of life invite him
 To abundant fruitage fair.
And beyond the opening glories
 Other, grander, summits rise,
Heights that hint yet broader vastness,
 Drinking joy of lovelier skies.

Here on earth the roses wither,
 But they ever bloom above ;
And forever there the lilies
 Breathe the sweetness of their love !
In the forest aisles of heaven
 Birds, and brooks, and zephyrs sing
Of the beauty and the grandeur
 Of the country of the King.

And His angels there rejoicing
 So attune their hearts to song
That the hills and forests vibrate
 With the tide that thrills along.
And the music of the numbers
 Of the minstrelsy on high

Shall intensify and sweeten
    Through the ages of the sky !

And from some bright summit yonder˜
    Where eternal splendors glow,
Shall the good man view the region
    Of his struggles here below !
O ! the retrospect from heaven
    That awaits the glorified,
Where, beyond death's darkened river,
    Morning gilds the other side !

And there'll be reunions yonder
    Of those death has sundered here ;
There again the light of faces
    That so many smiles endear !
And the well-remembered voices
    That entranced the other days
Shall be sweet in reminiscence
    Of the old familiar ways.

Voices have new charms in heaven,
    But they still remain the same—
Sweeter, dearer, for transition

From the life from which they came—
Yet enchanting with the accents
    That delighted days gone by
And gave omen, thus, aforetime,
    Of their cadences on high.

Faces there will be remembered
    By the features known before,
More of spirit there revealing,
    Radiant on the heavenly shore,
Yet the same familiar faces
    By the earthly memories dear—
Faces known and loved up yonder
    For the smiles they gave us here !

Constant over death's dark river
    Shine the lustrous stars of love,
And to cheer the good man hover
    Angels missioned from above !
Fares he onward and emerges
    From the darkness and the tide,
Where, beyond the shadowy river,
    Morning gilds the other side !

THE COUNTRY OF THE GOOD.

O YE pilgrims through this province
  To the kingdom of the Lord,
Fear not, though there is a river
  That your way worn feet must ford.
O ye pilgrims, dare those waters !
  Journey bravely through the flood,
For the trial of that fording
  Is the last one for the good !

Onward, pilgrims, though before you
  Flows the chilling tide of death ;
For beyond it is the country
  Of eternal bloom and breath !
Fear not, pilgrims, onward bravely,
  Onward through the icy flood,
For beyond that final fording
  Is the country of the good !

And the Mighty will be with you,
  To uphold you with His arm ;
And no wave shall overwhelm you,

Nor shall evil spirits harm.
And the angels will be waiting
To receive you from the flood
To the bliss of heavenly morning
In the country of the good !

There are youth and growth in heaven,
Youth grown wise and age grown young ;
There the crowns rewarding crosses,
There the sweet from bitter wrung ;
There companionship of spirits,
There the bliss of solitude ;
O ! the joy of even thinking
Of the country of the good !

And the joys of heaven shall heighten
All the shining ages through ;
Friends to friends will there be loyal,
Souls to souls will there be true ;
For, O bliss beyond description !
Souls by souls are understood
In the land beyond the fording,
In the country of the good.

THROUGH THE SHADOWS.

THERE'S no sun to cheer the valley
　　Where death's chilling waters flow ;
And of coast and clime beyond it
　　Those on this side do not know.

Birds sing not above those waters ;
　　There mysterious ravens chant,
Giving earth nor name nor inkling
　　Of the' land beyond their haunt.

Nothing grows by that cold river ;
　　And grew lily there or thorn,
Would it hint of what is yonder—
　　Boon or ban, or murk or morn ?

Yet must all go through that darkness,
　　Lighted by no cheering beam,
Through the waters and the shadows
　　That o'erhang the chilling stream.

For no bridge o'erspans that river,
　　Nor can mortals sail the wave ;
Nor can science guide the farer,
　　Or enhearten to be brave.

Nor can reason give the pilgrim
　　Boatman, compass or a barque;
Yet by faith he gains the daring
　　For the torrent and the dark.

Faith inspirits him with visions
　　Of the heaven of his quest,
Of the land beyond the shadows,
　　Of the country of the blest.

And right onward to that heaven,
　　Onward through the chilling stream,
Gladly, calmly, fares the pilgrim,
　　Couraged by faith's cheering beam,

Onward to eternal splendors
　　Where majestic mountains rise
In the radiance of the sunshine
　　Of the country of the skies.

INTERCESSION.

SAINTS in heaven are ever praying
　　For the souls that struggle here,

And the Father makes them answer
    That He holds His children dear,
That He pities them and tempers
    For them all their varied woes,
That for them His gracious spirit
    Through creation flows.

Helping wearied ones to carry
    That which burdeneth the heart
And inspiriting the nerveless
    To enact the hero's part
And to gain, in fray appointed
    Unto all to meet in life,
Wisdom, equipoise and prowess
    Equal to the strife.

Saints in heaven are ever praying
    For the souls on earth who sigh ;
And to answer them the Father
    Bids His swiftest angels fly
Unto earth to seek the saddened,
    Not, perchance, to give relief,
But to strengthen them to conquer
    Cruel fiends of grief.

Glad the angels earthward hasten !
 Thrill the spiritless with might,
Till those timid at the outset
 Put their furious foes to flight,
And enhearten so their comrades .
 Unto valor in the fray
That what seemed foredoomed disaster
 Crowns with joy the day !.

O, ye saints in heaven praying,
 High example have ye there !
For the Christ who in the Garden
 Poured his passioned soul in prayer
And, amid the darkness dying
 That his enemies might live,
With his latest breath entreated
 Heaven to forgive,

Now above is interceding
 For the souls of earth who sigh—
There in heaven, though high exalted
 And the ruler of the sky,
There in heaven the Christ is praying
 For the souls that struggle here:

And for Him the Father holdeth
    All His children dear.

And for Him the angels hasten
    Bringing blessings here below ;
And because of Him who suffered
    Temper they each earthly woe.
Saints of earth and saints translated,
    Sing, O sing, the glorious worth
Of the Sovereign of heaven,
    Of the Lord of earth.

LOVE PIECES.

III.

"COME, HAPPY BIRD."

COME, happy bird of sweetest note,
    Blithe bird of brightest wing,
Of one who close resembles thee
    Thy choicest matin sing.

She charms her home, as thou thy bower,
    With liquid warblings sweet,
And marks each hour with words sincere
    And winsome ways discreet.

Sing, bird, so bravely and so well
    That one who seeks her hand
Shall be inspired to speak and act
    The bravest in the land.

For only thus shall he attain
    To favor in her eyes,
Who but withholds, that he may win,
    What he esteems a prize;

While hers is modest estimate
    Of worth she may possess,
As thine, sweet warbler, of thy songs,
    His listening ears that bless.

Come, happy bird of sweetest note,
 Blithe bird of brightest wing,
Of one who close resembles thee
 Thy choicest matin sing !

ZEPHYRS.

YE zephyrs, bring the odors sweet
 That on your fragrant way ye meet,

Where all the rarest blooms combine
To make the air so near divine

It seems as if to earth were given
The flavors of the hills of heaven !

But can ye tell her breath who came
To wake his heart to purest flame

That ever burned in Valor's breast
When fortune smiled upon his quest?

Her words were music, ways were grace,
And calm on that expressive face

There glowed the hope of summer skies ;
While in the glancing of those eyes,

Which heralded intensest kiss
That ever warmed a heart to bliss,

A spirit shone that would inspire
The gods to their divinest fire !

Ye airs excelling any word
That earth or Eden ever heard ;

Ye zephyrs chanting numbers high,
To challenge harpers of the sky

Till they attempt sublimest song
That ever thrilled the heavenly throng—

Nor ye, nor they, can sing above
The music of that wondrous love !

THE SWEETHEART.

SO bold, should one of you accuse
    That some sweet girl inspires my muse,
To all the rest it would be news,
            But not to me.

The maiden never tells the fact
By any word or any act,
Evincing such consummate tact
      To keep it hid,

She is not reckoned on the list
Of those who try to "keep it whist,"
And in the search she might assist
      And none surmise

There was a reason for the zest
Wherewith she aided in the quest
To which the searchers had addressed
      Their skill in vain.

Keeping the secret a little more,
We twain, as others have before,
Will seek the parson's friendly door,
      And tell it there.

"MAIDEN DISCREET."

MAIDEN discreet, I give thee praise
  For words select and comely ways,

And wish thee many joyous days,
    And worthy friends.

May Honor win, by grand address,
The blissful good of thy caress,
And True Love come, thy heart to bless,
    And Hope to cheer.

For all like thee discreetly kind
May every cloud be silver-lined ;
For them be thornless roses twined,
    And evergreen.

NECTAR.

THE fools may laugh, the prudish quaff
    Their cups of pale cold mist,
And seem content with no more meant
    Than if two icebergs kissed !

Whoever thinks when Ellen drinks
    Her joy from Ronald's lips,
There's aught but love—that one above,
    At feasts where Juno sips

The nectar high that cheers the sky
    To its intensest glow,
Would deem such fire a dark desire
    And think the airs that blow

From paradise bring ill device,
    And kiss by angel given
Was wandering worse than that whose curse
    Sent Lucifer from heaven !

The fools may laugh, the prudish quaff
    Chill vapor of the morn,
Affecting stress of righteousness
    Which doth affection scorn—

Whoever thinks when Ronald drinks
    The joy by Ellen given
It is not well, would find it hell
    If he should get to heaven !

SATIRES.

IV.

SOME CRITICS.

THE wicked wish some critics have,
　　And knack and greed, to kill,
They think high evidence of taste
　　And proof of master skill.

To them all writers are at fault,
　　The finest paintings stuff,
And singers at their best too cheap
　　To honor with rebuff!

Yet may not pen, and brush, and harp
　　Still claim attention where
These critics should, of course, receive
　　By far the greatest share!

For were there none to paint or sing,
　　Or write in verse or prose,
What such as they would find to do
　　Is more than mortal knows.

They might ascend the upper spheres,
　　To criticise the stars
And teach good manners and good sense
　　To Jupiter and Mars,

Then clip away old Saturn's rings
    And set him bounds to run,
Or venture near the solar fires
    To regulate the sun !

And should they reach the better land,
    They would not blush to tell
The angels how to tune their harps
    To sing hosannas well ;

Nor for their colors to rebuke
    The alchemists of heaven,
Nor fail to painters there to say
    How poorly they had striven

In limning landscapes that entranced
    Apollo and his host,
While heavenly choirs from hymning turned,
    To wonder and to boast !

These critics would condemn the style
    In which the saints are dressed,
Insist on changes to improve
    The mansions of the blest,

And, raw recruits from earth, presume
    To dictate, there, on high,
The way archangels ought to wheel
    The armies of the sky,

And think themselves empowered to lead
    The squadrons sent afar
To subjugate rebellious worlds
    Or win a wayward star !

With coolness they descant upon
    The highest works of man,
And were creation built anew
    On a sublimer plan,

They yet would think the universe,
    Was theirs to criticise,
And would not fail to carp against
    The reconstructed skies !

IN AMBUSH.

THOUGH poisoned word be never heard,
    To voice the base designing
Ye contemplate on those ye hate,
    The thought does the maligning !

'Tis ever true, sin colors through
    And outward shows the staining
Of sin within, where sins begin ;
    And, slanderous words restraining,

If ye nurse aught of slanderous thought,
    That thought the victim curses ;
He vilifies by face and eyes,
    The evil thought who nurses.

His fellow-man he giveth ban
    Who casts the look suspicious ;
And if he praise, the cautious phrase,
    Rose-scented and judicious,

Belittles worse than open curse
    Of enemy malignant ;
And in his eyes are wily lies,
    Although he beam benignant.

These shall he send, to vex and rend
    The one his shrewdness blesses ;
They schooled the while to watch his smile,
    And kill whom he caresses.

HEART OF ICE.

WITHOUT, circumspect and sternly correct,
　　With character showing not any defect,
Thy coldness within, no luring can win ;
Pulseless, and therefore not given to sin !
Thou passionless one, what rivers can run
Where coldness turns backward the rays of the
　　　　sun ?
From sinning though free, what credit to thee?
So frigid art thou the tempter would flee,
Or, cold with concern, to ice-pillar turn
Where fiercest the fervors of hades should burn !

With forcefullest will, and busied to kill
The joy and the sweetness of others, until,
A-tremble with dread, around thee they tread,
With only the life to wish they were dead !
But cometh a day of contrasts that may
Melt all thy cold virtues to nothing away.
This warning dost spurn?—its truth thou shalt
　　　　learn
Where fiercer the fervors of hades shall burn
Than primal design of fiat divine—
For hell would be chilled with a presence like
　　　　thine !

WILLIAM WILLIAMS.

WHEN William Williams walks abroad
    He trips along so proud,
And steps so dainty on the street
    Rude people laugh aloud.

These lines expressive of regret
    That they should think to scorn
The man for whom the earth was made
    And stars the skies adorn !

For whom the summer solstice burns ;
    For whom the winter's cold,
The verdure of the pleasant spring,
    And autumn's red and gold !

A man of ancient family,
    Whom heraldry correct
Points backward to a crown and throne,
    Through ancestry direct !

And, still, when Williams walks abroad
    He has a gait so proud,
And steps so dainty on the street,
    The rude will laugh aloud !

TOMMY TRIM.

WHEN Tommy Trim at morning takes
    The pleasant train for town,
He wears the kids and hat correct,
    To match his whiskers brown.

And through the coaches every one,
    With equipoise of stride,
He walks, to throw from gorgeous eyes,
    Alternate to each side,

The glance benignant that shall cheer
    Those waiting till he bless
The hearts that thrill with agony
    For his high graciousness !

Ah, Tommy Trim ! remember well,
    The years will quickly fly
And kids will fade and time will dim
    The lustre of the eye !

And other ones with lovelier face
    And tuft of finer brown
Will smile, to win rewarding smiles
    From those who ride to town ;

And none recall, dear Tommy Trim,
  The matchless orbs of thine,
That beamed to cheer the other days
  With radiance benign !

OTHER POEMS.

V.

"MOST BEAUTIFUL RIVER."

MOST beautiful river of all that have sung
  Since music aforetime in Eden was young,
Thy waters, though charming, have cadence of
      grief,
And, chanting of trouble that finds no relief,
Speak under the joy of the notes of the song,
That somewhere the key-note of being is wrong,
That somewhere far back in the course of the
      flight
Of things which the First Cause designed to go
      right,
Some tired of their orbit and went from the way,
Persisting thenceforward still farther to stray,
Till, stranded in wandering and dark with the
      gloom
Of the wreck of the wayward, they shook with
      their doom !

Thou river that singest the joy of a clime
Of Eden-like sweetness of earlier time,
Thou river that singest the first bliss of man,
That blessing was only precursor of ban !

And driven from Eden and vagrant o'er earth,
Man, sighing for solace and seeking for worth,
Found little good fruitage, but vastness of dearth.
Blight found he for wheat-fields, and crows for
      the corn,
Found frost blasting roses but pointing the thorn,
In all fields found nightshade, or thistles, or tares,
In all paths found pitfalls, or quicksand, or snares,
Found fevers in cold airs and fevers in heats,
Found poisons in acids and poisons in sweets!
Found scarcely a gold grain, found little but
      dross,
Found life full of struggle, disaster 'and loss!

O, tell me, bright river, O, hear the complaint
That tortures the ages and notes their attaint,
That gives them no day-dawn, but deepens their
      gloom,
O, tell me, bright river, the cause of the doom!
What is it that burdens and worries in spite
Of solace of song of the rivers that quite
Would antidote seem in their charm of delight
For deepest and harshest and darkest of ban
That fiends could invent for the torture of man?

And singest thou, river, 'tis Sin that has done
The mischief, the havoc wrought under the sun?
Then tell me, bright river, for rivers must know
That sing of the unseen as onward they flow,
O, tell me why Sin and its consequent woe—
Why Sin after rightness and woe after bliss?
O, why, after Eden, misfortune like this,
That worries and saddens the men of the earth
And burns out its best fields to deserts of dearth?
Since blessing beforehand but deepens the curse,
Since sweet before bitter makes bitter the worse,
O, tell me, bright river, O, tell me, I pray,
If night was to be, O, why was there day?
O, tell me, bright waters, if tell me ye can,
O, why was there Eden as prelude to ban?

And sayest thou, river, that evil was given
To teach earth, by contrast, the value of heaven?
To warn man and spur him away from the bad,
And teach him through sadness, the way to be
        glad?
And if it was discipline meant by this grief,
O, why not some angel to teach such belief?
To sing unto earth that the thought in all this

Was only to heighten the chances for bliss?
That, covert in curses, hid blessings were given
To aid in the quest and the climbing for heaven?

And singest thou, river, of One who was sent
To tell what this sadness and mystery meant,
To lead man away from the cause of his woes
And aid him to conquer the ills that oppose?
The ban had so blinded that only in years
Could any be won from the cause of their tears.

Yet why this repining, O river of song?
Wrong cannot be righted by naming it wrong.
If problem it once was why man at the first
Was kept from the reason why he had been
      cursed,
At last by his troubles well visioned is he;
Misfortune has schooled him until he can see
The reason his day into darkness was turned;
Disaster has disciplined till he has learned,
That blessing is baneful unless it is earned,
That bitter beforehand but sweetens the cup,
When valiant the brave man drinks bitterness up,
That doubt when well mastered is loyal to hope,

That torture if conquered equips for emprise,
And hell if subjected gives road to the skies !

Then carol, ye waters, as glad as ye can ;
O, sing of the Eden that was before ban,
Ere man had been tempted to wander away
Or night came at morning, to darken his day !
Ere thistles outgrew the best blossoms of earth
And rich meads were turned into deserts of
        dearth !
And sing, O ye waters, as glad as ye can,
That those who learn well in the school of this ban
Shall somewhere out yonder find Eden for man,
With streams even sweeter than rivers that sung
Entrancing that Eden where music was young !

"BRIGHT ON YOUR NATIVE HILLS."

BRIGHT on your native hills
    The sun benignant beams,
Perennial down the pleasant slopes
    Still sing the happy streams,
Which feed yon river's tide that flows

In beauty through the vale ;
'Transparent, purling brooks
    Which sing of springs that never fail ;
And grand the mountains stand, as erst
    When there your kindred dwelt,
And fresh the mountain winds as airs
    Their fields and forests felt.

And ye remain to keep their homes,
    And guard the noble name
Earned by their share of those grand deeds
    That give New England fame.
Shines their example, still, as bright
    As beams the golden sun ;
Flows still-their influence as pure
    As mountain waters run.
So cherish ye the fame they gained,
    And emulate their worth,
Your names, when ye are gone, shall live,
    Perennial in the earth !

"SING, BIRD OF CHEER."

WHILE cheering light
    Of morning bright

O'er eastern height is glowing,
 And choicest flowers
 In any bowers
Or any landscape growing,
 Their sweets exhale,
 To fill the gale
Soft on the valley blowing,
 Thou sweetest bird
 Mine ears have heard,
Whose liquid music, flowing,
 Hath magic charms
 To still alarms,
The sweetest peace bestowing,

 On fleetest wing
 Fly thou and sing,
To cheer a brave heart bearing
 A load of grief
 Beyond belief,
Beyond an angel's daring ;
 Though worn and faint,
 Giving no plaint,
But brave on life's road faring ;
 Through griefs, discreet,

With spirit sweet,
Well worth an angel's sharing.
Sing, bird of cheer,
So he shall hear
Above earth's loudest blaring.

And sing again
To cheer him, when
Noon's fervid heats are burning ;
Assure him well
That thou wilt tell,
Ere next the noon's returning,
In thy best tune,
That some sweet boon
Shall soothe the plaintive yearning
Of his sad heart,
As he, the art
Of grand endurance learning,
Seeks only joy
Which doth not cloy,
All vain enjoyment spurning.

Then, sweetest bird
Mine ears have heard,

When sunset's wealth is streaming,
   In western skies,
   To glad the eyes
And set the spirit dreaming
   Of Ind of old
   And towers of gold
With heavenly splendors beaming,
   Sing once again,
   And tell him when,
Thy pledge in truth redeeming,
   Thou bringest joy,
   It shall not cloy
Nor be less than its seeming !

THE ANTIDOTE.

EXPECT to give the doubting faith?
   As well to give the lungless breath !
As well to give the eyeless ken,
Or reason unto mindless men.
O ye of earth whom angels tell
The precious art of keeping well,
O ye above, whom stars and sky
Have taught the alchemies on high,

And unto whom the power is given
To study trees and blooms of heaven
And learn what essences have they
That ills of mortals will allay
And send these qualities in dews
That shall their potencies infuse
In herbage here for man to use,
To aid him to regain the wealth,
The boon, the blessing of his health—
Ye sapient ones of earth and sky,
If here 'tis known, or if on high,
The antidote for doubt declare,
The medicine to cure despair !

THE PROBLEM.

HERE wailing a moment, then struggling a day,
  Not wishing the contest but forced to the fray,
Man dying of combating ills of this life
Or dying of joy of achieving the strife,
Leaves here where he struggled some ounces of
        clay,
While all that informed it is wafted away—

A ghost gone to some land, and what land who
    knows?
With spirits congenial, or those who are foes?
Where bleak over wide wastes blow chill damps of
    death?
Or where from fierce furnaces hate's heated
    breath?
Where skies shed the sweetness and brightness of
    heaven?
Or where o'er the concave grim war clouds are
    driven?
O! wherefore begun life? and what is its end?
Whence came it? what means it? and whereto the
    trend?

THE BRIGHT BELIEF.

IF, sore discouraged and distressed,
    With sorrows and with cares oppressed,
And sins confessed, and unconfessed,
    And every ill,

The heart were struggling for relief,

And found no succor from its grief,
In buoyant trust, and bright belief, —
    How sad the earth !

But rules reverse of these obtain,
Nor mortal suffered yet in vain,
A trivial, nor the largest pain,
    Nor ever will.

So let the troubled take new heart,
Learn well of suffering the art,
Nor shun to share a generous part
    In life's good griefs !

For none hath God the tender care
He ever shows for those who bear
Of life's worst woes abundant share,
    Enduring well.

O ! ever blessed bright belief !
That joy which cometh after grief,
Is sweetest joy, and is not brief,
    Like other joys !

Inspiring, grand, and true, the thought,
That bliss by bitter trials bought,

Is nearer unto heaven than aught
  On earth beside.

And there, beyond thine earthly ban,
The wisdom of His rounded plan
Who ordereth the ways of man
  Shall be made plain ;

And thou shalt know thy Father spoke,
When fates thy noblest planning broke
And gave to thee a cross and yoke—
  That prove thy crown !

"THOU SHALT DISCERN."

DESPITE the darkness and the din,
  And all the tendencies to sin
    Thou findest here,

Earth is the place and now the time,
To win the boon of happy chime
  For that Beyond,

Where, if thou rightly livest here,
Thou shalt discern, with vision clear,
    The meaning high

Of all the mysteries of earth,
And find those things had real worth
    That useless seemed,

And, grateful, thank the Eternal Mind,
That He, the Infinite, the Kind,
    Hath planned it all !

BLESS THY KIND.

O BLESS thy kind, and unto thee
  Shall angels chant the minstrelsy

Far sweeter than the singing heard
From any brook or any bird

In happiest glen of all the world,
And sweeter than the brooks that purled

In Eden when the earth was young
And all the stars together sung !

And dost thou doubt, and point to men
Who bless and are not blessed again,

But live in grief, and grieving die
Of much bestowing charity?—

Perhaps not here, yet in some clime,
Perhaps not now, yet some good time

Of God's sure years, shall greet the eye
That moistens here with sympathy,

Scenes bright as those the seer of eld
Entranced on Patmos isle beheld,

When full the radiant glories shone
From gates, and temple, and the Throne !

And grander shall the music be
Of that good time than minstrelsy

Of Eden when the earth was young
And all the stars together sung.

DOMINANT.

WHEN, dominant by warring well
      And in the fight grown strong,
The soul reigns o'er the outer self
      That held it subject long,

With power and poise there's vision given
      To see what meaneth life,
And, in the triumph gained, to read
      The reason for the strife.

Then bright on life's dark mystery
      The stars of promise rise,
To glow until fruition's day
      Shall break along the skies !

Forever lustrous are those stars,
      That mortals may discern ;
Yet only visioned souls can see
      Their constant glories burn !

Fight on, O man, until thy soul
      Full visioned is, and strong,
And regnant o'er the outer self
      That held it subject long.

VICTOR.

WHEN woes are more than words can tell
    Or human bravery bear,
O Thou who doest all things well,
    Inspire till through Thy care

The soul those griefs shall dominate
    And, by the trial strong,
Envoke from dissonance of fate
    The melody of song,

And excellence of vigor gain
    To meet what ills oppose,
And fortitude to suffer pain
    Till bliss from anguish grows,

And springs within the purpose high
    Of that true graciousness
Which quickly hears if sorrow cry
    And hastens forth to bless.

When woes are more than words can tell
    Or human bravery bear,
The soul, O Lord, endures them well
    That hath Thy gracious care.

IN sunny days of childhood playing,
    When life was all one scene of Maying,
And thou hadst not a thought of straying,
    God blessed thee then.

Forgiving all thy youthful sinning,
He helped thee to a manly winning
Good triumphs o'er a bad beginning,
    And helps thee still,

That, in the strife which ceaseth never,
Demanding watch and warring ever,
Thou do, by manliest endeavor,
    The victor be.

A ROSE.

BEYOND the single rose he sought,
    She piled the offering high
Of lily, pink and jessamine
    And larkspurs of the sky,

Until the gift, full antidote
    For all his grief and strife,
Led him to bless, with what she gave,
    Another troubled life.

And words for his bestowment said
    Were finer fragrance far
Than concentrated odors breathed
    From all the lilies are.

Ah, lady, acts like thine shall bloom
    In choicest beauty where
The sweetness from the heavenly plains
    Perfumes the sentient air.

THE IDEAL.

REDUCE to fact your fancy,
    Nor tarry till you do
Make real the ideal
    That God has given you.

Most real the ideal,
    Least fact what most call fact ;
And of ideal most real,
    Ideal in an act.

INTUITIONS.

Follow thine intuitions,
   They always lead thee right;
In all of thine ambitions
   Obey the inner light.

Whatever to thy vision
   Seems duty, bravely do,
Albeit fierce derision
   The doing leads thee through.

And when of ease Elysian
   Appears alluring view,
Then quick to the monition
   Thou hear'st within be true.

Intensify decision
   To follow still the right;
And onward to thy mission,
   With vigilance and might.

Thus heeded, intuitions
   Shall ever lead thee right—
To crowns for the ambitions
   True to the inner light.

O GIVEN by fiends the gall to drink,
    And sweeter grown for all they send ,
A kind and watchful Providence
    Will soon proclaim the ordeal's end ;
Yet call thee not from earth above,
    But ask thee, wearied one, take rest ;
And that thy restless eyes may close,
    Command that, from the roseate west,
Angels reposeful influence sweet
    Pour forth, to give thy spirit calm,
And others send, on zephyrs borne,
    To soothe thy troubled heart with balm.

Angelic ones shall sentinel
    Thy rest, and fragrance waft till day,
Shall brightly break and bid thee, glad,
    Thy grateful orisons to pay ;
Refreshed, inhale the ambrosial air
    And walk beneath a happy sky,
Inspired, by carol of the birds
    And songs of brooks that murmur by,
With faith that Heaven will bless thy days,
    Each westering sun bring peaceful sleep,

And every morn new evidence
 That angels tender watch-care keep !

Heroic sufferer, who hast borne
 The burden of a broken heart,
Patiently, artlessly, and yet
 With all the dignity of art,
While so intent to bless the world
 None knew what woes thine own heart had—
Deep, bitter griefs, which, told above,
 Would make the heavenly singers sad,—
Soon shalt thou learn the gracious truth,
 Through griefs and cares, which here annoy,
Heaven builds the path by which thy feet
 Shall reach the highest hills of joy !

BUILDING.

WHEN some kind voice tells thee plainly
 Of new building for thine hand ;
And thou findest hindrance mainly
 In the strangeness of command

Calling thee from routine labor
 In the wonted, humble, sphere,

And thou fear'st from foe or neighbor
    An unkind or jealous sneer ;

Do not for such hindrance smother
    That sweet voice that speaks within ;
Thou mayst find the foe turn brother,
    If thou manfully begin,

And continue bravely doing,
    Work the angel bids thee do ;
And, each day the work renewing,
    Thou shalt find it ever new.

It shall charm like high romances,
    Gemming legends of old days ;
And, beyond thy farthest fancies,
    O'er wide plains, by untrod ways,

Paths unknown to other leaders,
    Angel guide shall lead thee sure,
For the gold and goo lly cedars
    Which shall evermore endure,

In the towers of consummation
    That shall mark thy work complete,

And call forth the world's laudation,
    Which thy shrinking ears shall greet.

Fear not but for all these praises
    That Good Power shall well prepare,
Who hath life in all its phases
    Under His benignant care.

For, by thorns and frequent crosses,
    Which thy heart shall fully test,
Sad reverses and sore losses,
    If His wisdom thinketh best,

Unto meekness He will hold thee,
    Still commanding thee, be brave,
And obey injunctions told thee
    By the angel that He gave.

And this angel shall sustain thee,
    Be the work or long or hard ;
And the future shall explain thee,
    All that did thy work retard

Was designed to bid thee stronger
    Make the building of thine hand,
Which, than time's duration longer,
    Through eternity, shall stand.

ACKNOWLEDGEMENT.

ACCEPT, selectest man I know,
    Who met my sadder years,
And all uumindful of thy griefs
    Wast mindful of my tears,
Whose kindness when but few were kind
    And noble gentleness
Were so inspiring and so grand
    And royally did bless,

Accept the gratitude, too small,
    My heart would offer thee
For thine example and thine aid
    So freely granted me—
The heartiest words and kindest deeds
    Wisely, but freely, given,
Imparting to my bitterest hours
    A foretaste of my heaven!

Once, scorned by those whom I had blessed,
    And doubted for my trust,
My pleasant plans were broken all,
    My hopes were in the dust.
Then thou didst cheer me—blessed hour!

And sacred be the spot,
When those ignoble men are both
    Forgiven and forgot !

AT SCHOOL.

AFFLICTION is the school wherein
    Gains character new power,
And excellence, by fighting sin,
    Wins an abundant dower.

WARRING.

WHO wars for right, hope well befits ;
    To him the stars are true ;
For him there's always Austerlitz,
    And never Waterloo !

OUR FAITH IN MEN.

ENNOBLING is our faith in men ;
    It lifts us from the dust,
And what we trust a man to be,
    We make the man we trust.

MY NATIVE LAND.

GOD bless the land where I was born
    And played a happy child,
Ere yet I saw a southern swamp
    Or roamed a western wild,

And where, within the glens among
    The Massachusetts hills,
My early being was attuned
    By cadence of the rills.

O ! could I be forgiven, did
    My heart not turn to thee
With gratitude and pride, dear land,
    For all thou art to me?

Thine atmosphere and scenery,
    Thy present and thy past,
Thy people and their freedom's wealth,
    To last while time shall last.

And all along the coming years,
    Where'er my pathway lies,
Whatever lot is meted out,
    Or kind or cold my skies,

Still, evermore, my song, at home,
 Or on a foreign strand,
Through life and at the closing hour,
 God bless my native land !

And if the Powers above shall grant
 The boon of heavenly rest,
"Twill sweeten even that to know
 My native land is blessed.

"PRIZE THOU THYSELF."

O, BLEST with innocence and health,
 'And wisdom far above thy years,
Who hast not felt heart-rending griefs,
 Nor wept the bitter, scalding tears,—

Exquisite maiden, whose bright ways
 Are pride of her wh) thee did bear,
And who, these years, with tender hand,
 Hath nurtured thee with fondest care,—

Prize thou thyself, thy kindred prize,
 Thy home and all its quiet joys ;

And keep thee, much as in thee lies,
    From earth's frivolity and noise.

Cherish the gift of thy good sense,
    And do thou bravely live and keep
Thy soul from all that causes shame
    And makes the watching angels weep !

For thee, God grant the kindest skies,
    For thee, sincerest, noblest friends ;
For thee, all earth's substantial good,
    And heaven, when earth's ordeal ends.

For him whose worth deserves thy heart,
    And whose brave ways thy heart shall win,
May brightest stars benignant beam,
    For him, and all his noble kin.

O, blest with innocence and health,
    And wisdom far above thy years,
Thy heart be long unknown to grief,
    And long thine eyes unknown to tears !

"SHE PLACED THE BITTER-SWEET."

TO girlhood's home returning,
    She placed the bitter-sweet

Within the ancient mansion,
  Where sunbeams shadows meet ;

And there declared : "Henceforward
  Bé kindness all my theme ;
With constant hand dispensing,
  The moments to redeem ;

"Teaching, if I have suffered,
  I would the world be blest ;
Praying, if I have struggled,
  The weary have good rest.

"I thank Thee, Heavenly Father—
  My name Thou hast kept sweet,
And through these bitter trials,
  Hast kept my ways discreet."

To girlhood's home returning,
  She placed the bitter-sweet
Within the ancient mansion,
  Where sunbeams shadows meet.

INTO THE SUNSHINE.

AWAY from doubts that chill and blight,
  Into the joy of faith's clear light,
Away from doubts that chill and blight !

Come to the sunshine bringing bloom—
For the rose there's always room ;
Come to the sunshine bringing bloom.

Into the sunshine of belief
Lead thou the stricken sons of grief,
Into the sunshine of belief;

Into the sunshine, with a song,
To cheer their faltering steps along ;
Into the sunshine with a song.

Give them the sunshine of your trust ;
If they have joy you surely must
Bestow the sunshine of your trust.

Live in the sunshine while you live,
And unto all your sunshine give ;
Live in the sunshine while you live.

And then beyond the stars and sun,
Shalt thou with all thy toiling done,
In some good land beyond the sun,

Beyond the doubts that chill and blight,
Abide in the unceasing light,
Beyond the doubts that chill and blight !

"GOOD-BYE, SWEET STARS."

SWEET stars, what high delight
  Is vigil in the night
Your lustre maketh bright.
But now a hand unbars
The morn—good-bye, sweet stars.
Good-bye—nay, linger still ;
Shed ye your radiance till
Once more I drink your glow :
Then stars, ye sweet stars, go,
If go, sweet stars, ye must ;
And, bright, sweet stars, I trust
Your vows to come again ;
And then, dear stars, and then !
But now a hand unbars
The morn—good-bye, sweet stars !
Yet, stay, for stars are given
To ken the truths of heaven—

O stay, and teach that good,
That high beatitude,
The best of all belief,
That joy succeeds to grief.
O best of all good gain,
The bliss that grows from pain—
Possession come from loss,
And crown that follows cross !
Despair ! endeavor, hope :
The slough—-the heavenly cope !

When all the skies are dark,
And there's no glory spark
To gem the firmament
And hint of Heaven's intent
Of blessing unto man,
Nor shadow forth the plan —
The spirit can discern
Your stellar fervors burn,
In proof that still above
Presides the Heavenly Love.

And, now, sweet stars, a hand
As by magician's wand

The gates of morn unbars !
Good-bye, sweet stars, sweet stars !
Ye go, and I may rest,
With dreamless slumber blest,
A few brief hours of morn.
And then, where flowers adorn
The meadows and the hills,
I'll join the birds and rills,
To sing, ye stars, your praise—
Accept, ye, then, the lays.
For ye can hear, I ween,
And see, when all unseen
And all unheard—when day
Hath sent ye far away.
And when again ye shine,
Teach me the hand divine
That now the morn unbars—·
Good-bye, sweet stars, sweet stars !

www.ingramcontent.com/pod-product-compliance
Lightning Source LLC
Chambersburg PA
CBHW020026030726
47499CB00007B/2294